JONAH AND THE FISH

written by **DANDI DALEY MACKALL**
illustrated by **LISSY MARLIN**

flipside
STORIES

TYNDALE HOUSE PUBLISHERS, INC.
CAROL STREAM, IL

To Ellie Hendren,
with love forever!

Visit Tyndale's website for kids at www.tyndale.com/kids.

TYNDALE is a registered trademark of Tyndale House Publishers, Inc. The Tyndale Kids logo is a trademark of Tyndale House Publishers, Inc.

Jonah and the Fish

Copyright © 2016 by Dandi A. Mackall. All rights reserved.

Illustrations copyright © Lissy Marlin. All rights reserved.

Designed by Jacqueline L. Nuñez

Edited by Stephanie Rische

Scripture quotations are taken from the *Holy Bible*, New Living Translation, copyright © 1996, 2004, 2015 by Tyndale House Foundation. Used by permission of Tyndale House Publishers, Inc., Carol Stream, Illinois 60188. All rights reserved.

For manufacturing information regarding this product, please call 1-800-323-9400.

ISBN 978-1-4964-1120-4

Printed in China

22	21	20	19	18	17	16
7	6	5	4	3	2	1

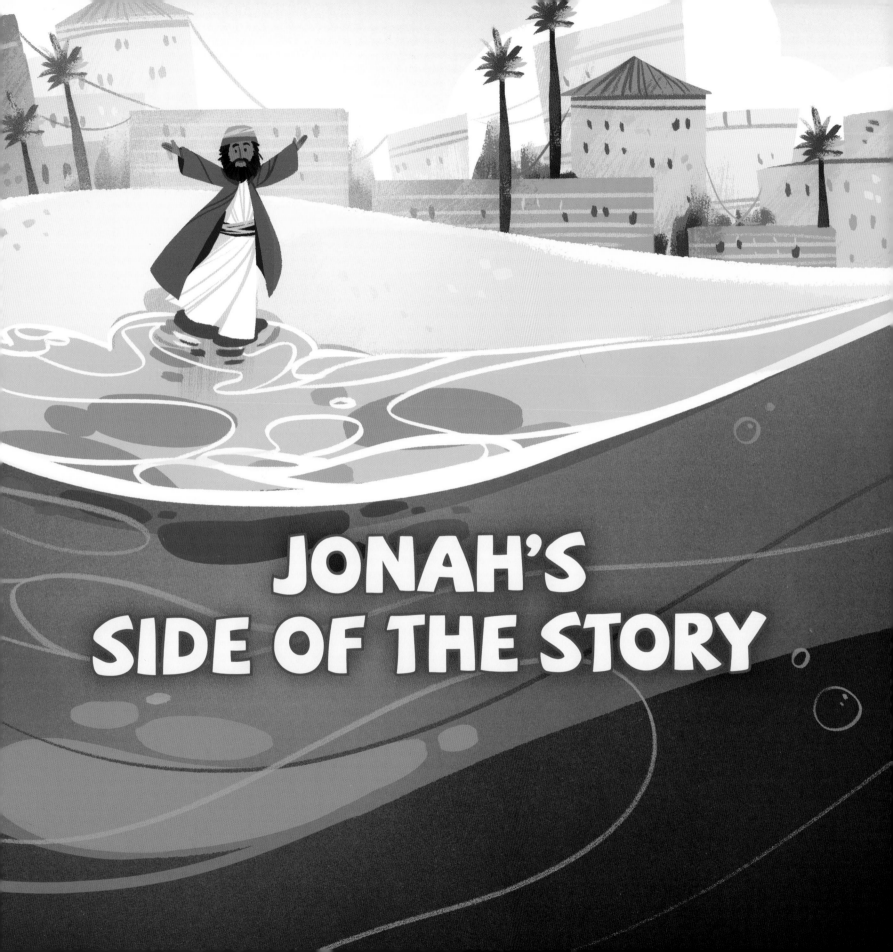

JONAH'S SIDE OF THE STORY

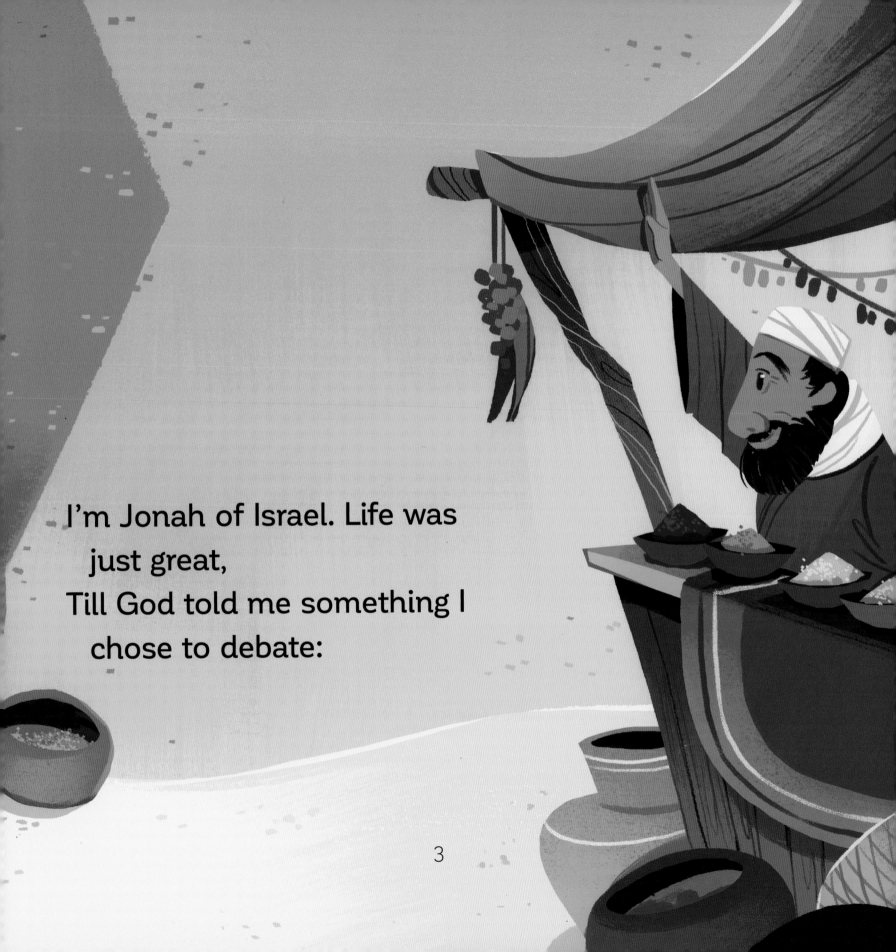

I'm Jonah of Israel. Life was just great,
Till God told me something I chose to debate:

"Now go up to Nineveh! Here's what to do:
Just tell them I love them the way I love you."

But I didn't like all those people up there.
So here's what I said: "God, I just do not care!"

5

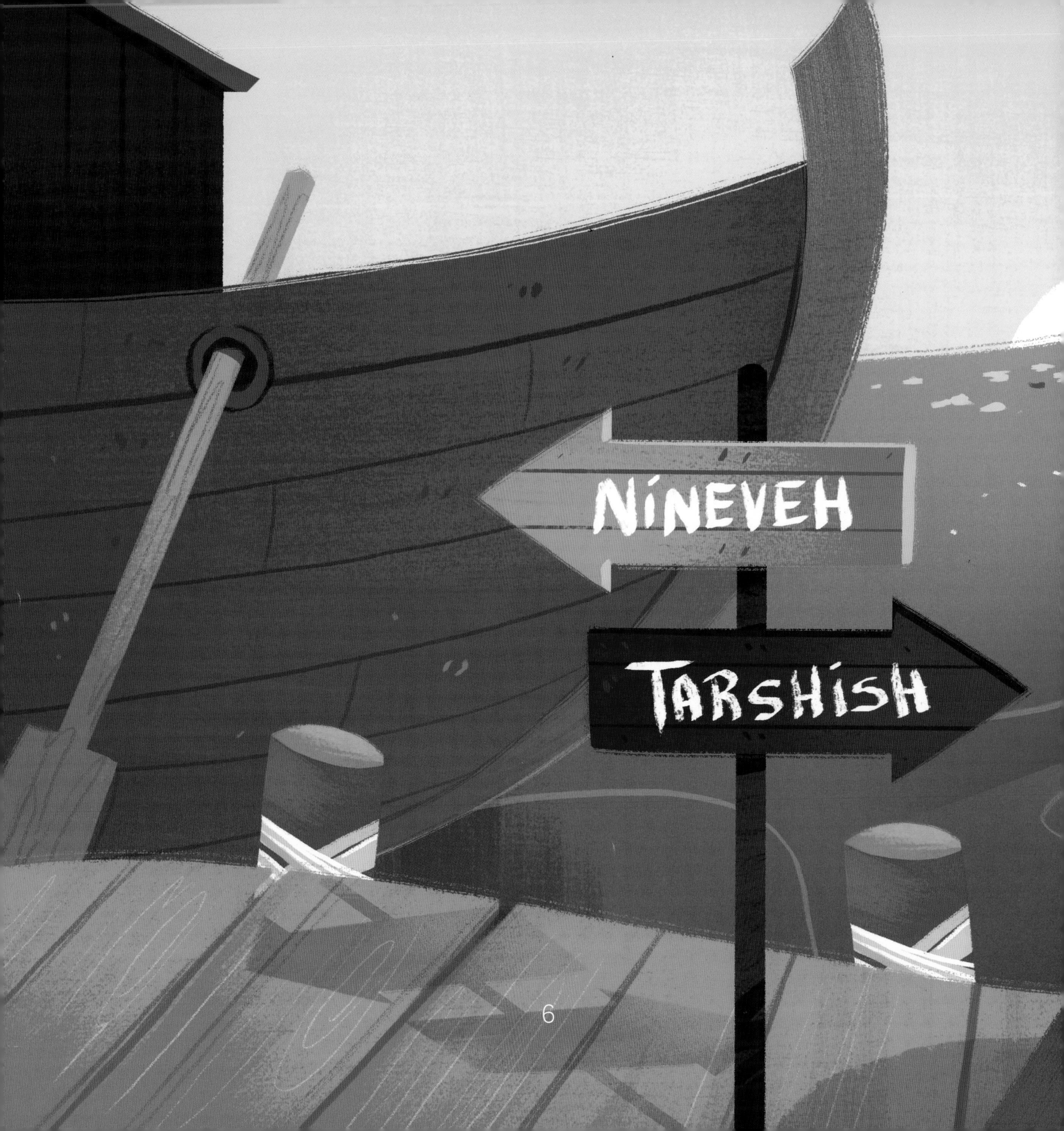
NINEVEH
TARSHISH

I bought me a ticket and
sailed on a ship—
The opposite way from
that Nineveh trip.

7

But God stirred the waves with a fierce storm at sea.
I told the ship's captain, "The problem is ME."

The sailors tossed cargo to lighten the load.
The harder the wind blew, the harder they rowed.

"You must throw me in, or you won't stay afloat!"

At last, the men tossed me right out of the boat.

I sank in the waters. Oh, why had I fled?
And that's when I saw a big fish straight ahead.

14

The fish swam right for me, its mouth open wide.
I slipped through its teeth—then I swooshed deep
  inside.

18

Day one, I was thinking, *My answer's still no.*
'Cause since I hate Nineveh, why should I go?

19

I came to my senses, I think, on day three.
I said I was sorry and begged God, "Send ME!"

That fish took a breath. Then I felt myself soar
UP, UP, like a dove, before landing on shore.

I waved to the fish, for I knew I'd been blessed.
I walked straight to Nineveh. God's way is best.

THE FISH'S
SIDE OF
THE STORY

I'm a mighty big fish in a mighty big sea.
There I lived and I ruled and I swam worry free.
But I thought I was born for a deed brave and bold,
And that deed hadn't come, though I'd grown very old.

Then a storm stirred the waves, and a howling wind blew.
And I spotted a ship with a terrified crew.
The waves rocked their boat. It could turn upside down!
Unless someone saved them, I feared they'd all drown.

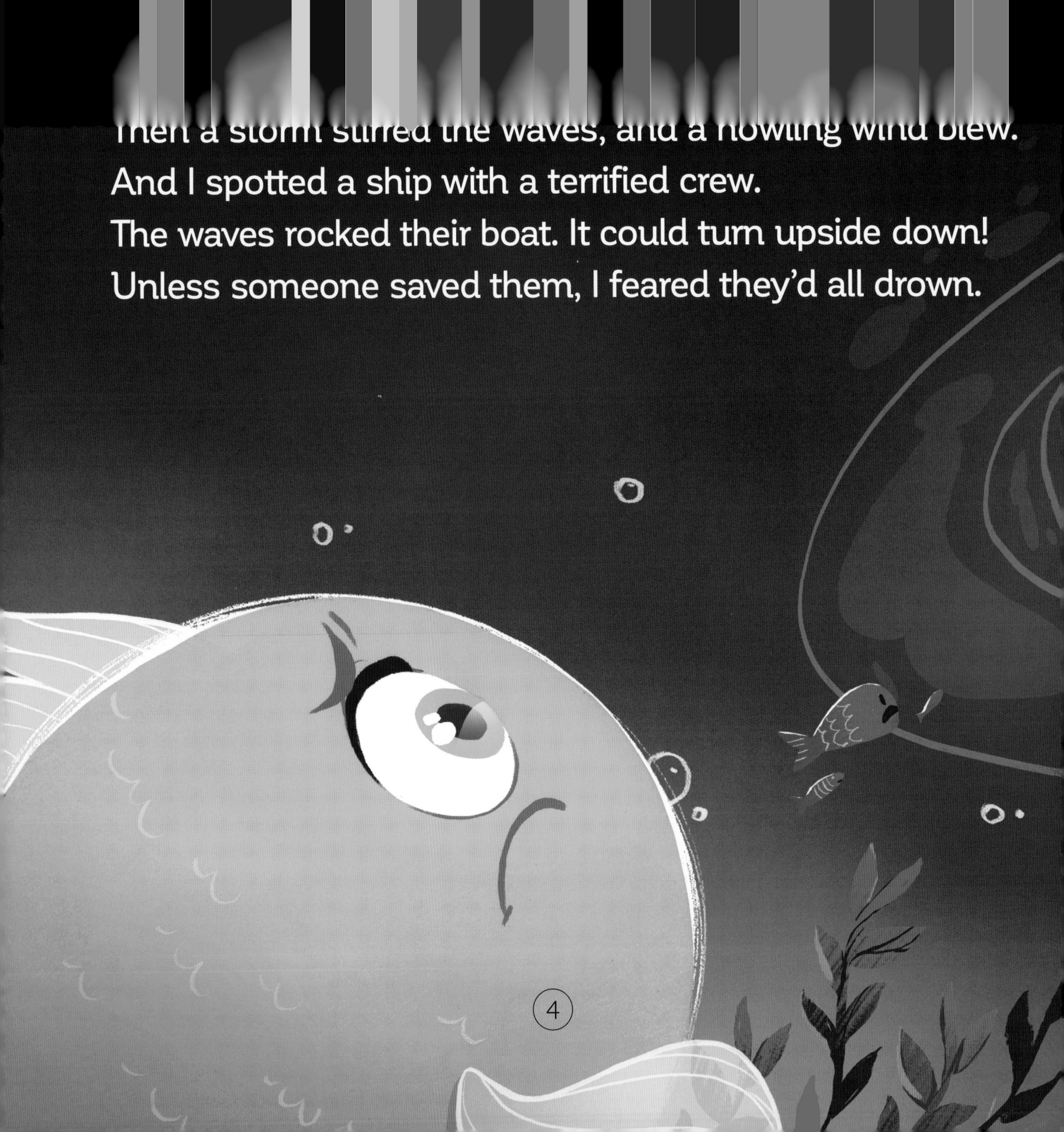

Then a voice I knew well said, "Today is the day!
Now the deed I've prepared will be coming your way!"
It was God, the Creator, who governs the seas.
I would heed His command, for I wanted to please.

Above, on the ship, someone prayed to the Lord.
Then down came a man who was tossed overboard!
I watched till I heard the Creator's strange plan:
"Your brave and bold deed is to swallow this man!"

But man is the highest of all
   God's creations!
I'd thought that my deed would
   bring great celebrations.

"Now, swallow this man, and
   your deed will begin!"
I opened my jaws,
   and the man
   slid on in.

11

That man kept his silence as day passed to night.
For three days I wondered if I had done right.
The man in my belly said nothing at all.
I feared that I'd only imagined God's call.

At last the man prayed, "Lord, I know what to do.

I'll go and tell Nineveh all about You!"

And that's when the Master said, "One command more:

Now spit this man, Jonah, out onto the shore!"

I laughed as I swam. Then I took a deep breath,
And up came the man, as if risen from death!
He landed—kerplop!—and he tumbled a bit.
Who knew my great deed would be SWALLOW AND
SPIT?

17

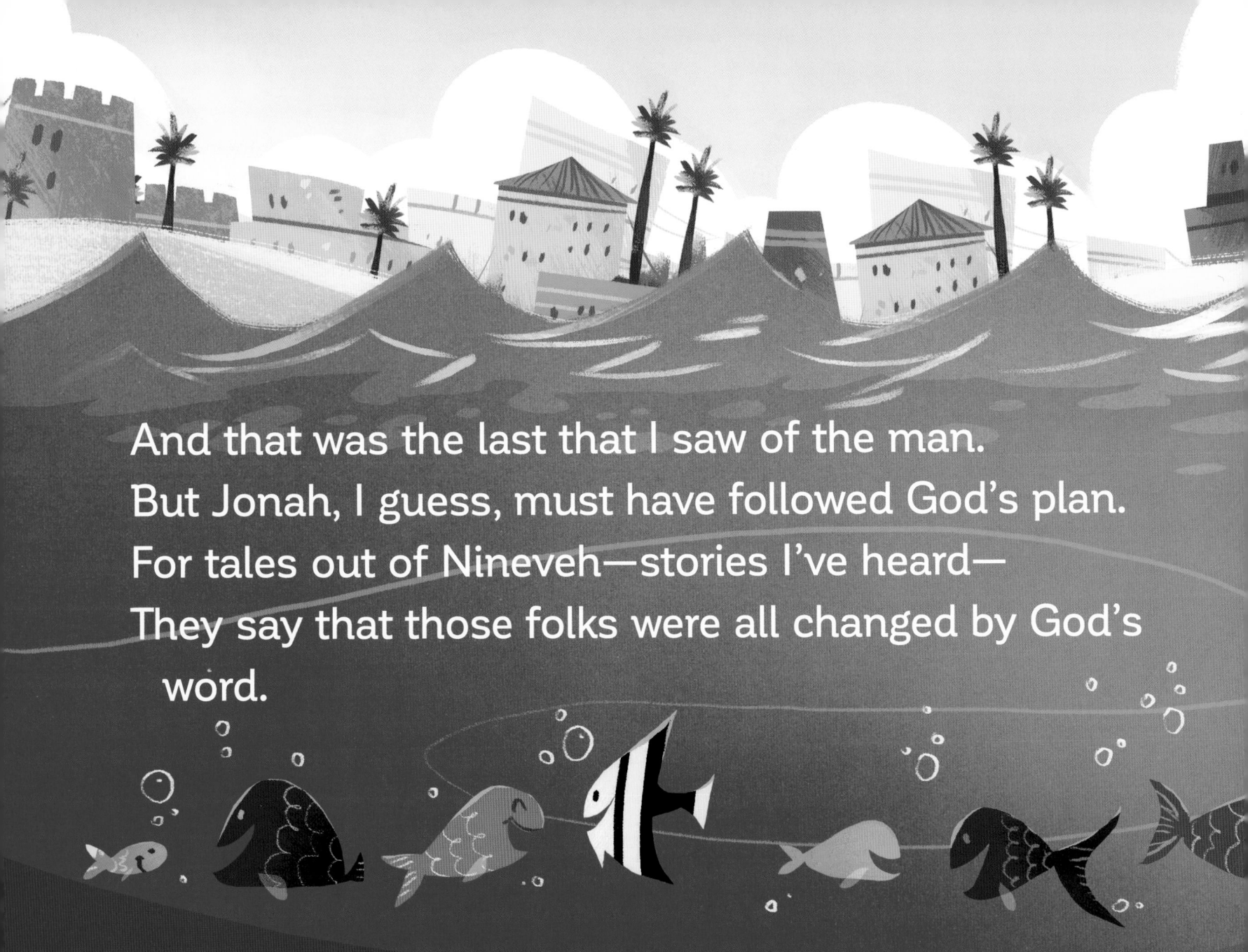

And that was the last that I saw of the man.
But Jonah, I guess, must have followed God's plan.
For tales out of Nineveh—stories I've heard—
They say that those folks were all changed by God's
   word.

The LORD said, . . . "Nineveh has more than 120,000 people living in spiritual darkness, not to mention all the animals. Shouldn't I feel sorry for such a great city?"

JONAH 4:10-11